The 9/11 Principal

# The 9/11 Principal

Gwendolyn Tose'-Rigell

Copyright © 2024 **Tose'-Rigell Publishing**

All rights reserved. No part of this publication may be reproduced, distributed, or transmitted in any form or by any means, including photocopying, recording, or other electronic or mechanical methods, without the prior written permission of the publisher, except in the case of brief quotations embodied in critical reviews and certain other noncommercial uses permitted by copyright law. For permission requests, write to the publisher, addressed "Attention: Book Rights and Permission," at the address below.

Published in the United States of America

ISBN 978-1-962110-97-6 (SC)
ISBN 978-1-962110-95-2 (HC)
ISBN 978-1-962110-96-9 (Ebook)

Tose'-Rigell Publishing
222 West 6th Street
Suite 400, San Pedro, CA, 90731
stoserig@gmail.com

Order Information and Rights Permission:

Quantity sales. Special discounts might be available on quantity purchases by corporations, associations, and others. For details, contact the publisher at the address above.

For Book Rights Adaptation and other Rights Permission. Call us at toll-free 1-888-945-8513 or send us an email at admin@stellarliterary.com.

CONTENTS

Introduction vii

Part 1 – Before September 1

Part 2 – September 11, 2001 23

Part 3 – Final Thoughts 29

Introduction

My mother, Gwendolyn Tose'-Rigell, had a unique vantage point on the morning of September 11, 2001. As the principal of Emma E. Booker Elementary School in Sarasota, Florida, she found herself in the company of the President of the United States as the catastrophic events began to unfold.

President George W. Bush was coming to their school that morning as part of his efforts to promote reading in schools. After weeks of anticipation and preparation, the excitement amongst the teachers, students, and staff was at a fever pitch.

Gwen wrote this account of her experiences shortly after 9/11. In it, she describes the time period beginning with the first phone call she received from the White House several months before the actual presidential visit. Her story includes all the preparation for the visit. It details what happened at the school on 9/11 from the time she welcomed the President Bush to the school until the time he was whisked away. Gwen also addresses a few of the rumors and distortions of fact regarding what really happened at Emma E. Booker that morning.

My mother always felt it was her responsibility to write about what she saw, thought, and felt as she watched as world-changing events unfolded that morning. Her dream was to someday share this account of what happened with others.

This book is the fulfillment of her dream, one she will surely be able to witness from heaven. After a long struggle with cancer, Gwen went to be with the Lord on December 26, 2007.

Stevenson Rigell

Part 1
Before September

I remember the first call well. I thought it was coming from a jokester. No principal gets a call from the office of the President of the United States (POTUS) saying the President is interested in visiting your school—but call they did. Someone, whose voice I had never heard before, asked some preliminary questions, kind of like a screening. The caller referred to an event; potential visit, that much was certain. Looking back, nothing could have remotely prepared me for the events that would eventually take place that day or for the many days to follow. Following that initial call, literally months went by, four to be exact, and I never heard another word or received another call. Then, one day the phone rang and the person on the other end told me we were in the running. No decision has been made yet, but the president might be coming to your school. *Yeah, sure*, I thought, *and I'm the queen of England.*

A few weeks passed, and I assumed *The Emma* was no longer in the running. (For clarification, my staff and I refer to our school, Emma E. Booker Elementary, as *The Emma*.) That was fine to me; it was an honor to have even been considered. I saw it as a privilege to have even received the call, considering the thousands of schools the president had to choose from.

More time passed. One day in August our county superintendent of schools, Wilma Hamilton, stopped me in a meeting. She told me I needed to go back to my school shortly to receive a call from someone regarding a White House visit.

Outwardly, I tried to act cool and nonchalant. Inside, a mini-parade was going on, complete with a percussion session. My heart was bursting with pride. It didn't even matter that he was a Republican and I was a Democrat. The president was thinking about The Emma and that was all that mattered.

My immediate supervisor John Zoretich and the public relations person for the school district, Sheila Weiss, accompanied me back to the school. There was another period of waiting—then the phone rang. **It's official!** The Advance Team would be coming to pay The Emma a visit.

Cinderella didn't have anything on me at that moment. I could only imagine what she must have felt like preparing to meet with an audience so far removed from her daily environment.

Within a week I received yet another call, informing me that the Advance Team, (which they said would consist of *a few people*), would be coming to Sarasota just to assess the feasibility of a presidential visit taking place at our school. The team wanted to take a look at the facility, the layout of the grounds, to look around and ask me some more questions. The date was set, the meeting would be in my office, and we would go from there.

Now, I meet with people all the time. I'm a principal. I meet with teams of teachers, teams of parents, teams of students, teams of my peers and teams from companies. But no team meeting could have prepared me for *the Advance Team.*

Sheila Weiss, the Sarasota schools communications director, and I met with the Advance Team at the Emma. When they showed up that morning, it was obvious my office would not be large enough. We quickly proceeded to the Media Center where introductions began. Business cards were exchanged so Sheila and I would have an idea as to who did what. My mind was already too overloaded to remember anyone.

Sheila and I held our own. We sat listening and responding to the questions of the Advance Team. We listened to them asking questions amongst themselves. In my mind, I was calculating our taxpayer dollars at work. At the same time, I was thinking that maybe I was understaffed. There should be more people helping me do the tasks on my campus. The questions finally ended, and we left the Media Center. The Advance Team wanted to take a look at the location I had in mind for the reading initiative to take place. For me, there was only one possible choice. Since this was an elementary school in Florida, where I have yet to see an auditorium or gymnasium, the event could only take place in our cafeteria, which also served as the auditorium

The event was tentatively scheduled to take place early in the school day. My mind kept saying we would have to be in and out of the cafeteria pretty quickly that morning because we start feeding children at 10:30 a.m.

The cafeteria plan was soon scrapped. As the Advanced Team members stood on the stage, they decided the lighting would not be favorable to the president because it would make him look *too yellow.* My next thought was *it's probably ruining my color as well.* As a matter of fact, I'm sure I came right out and said that.

My issue, suddenly, was space; we needed enough space to include as many people from The Emma as possible in whatever area was chosen. The Advance Team chose the Media Center. Mind you, this was still all preliminary, but at least the location had tentatively been selected. That was only the beginning of my work with the Advance Team. Each member of that team was responsible for one thing and one thing only. I learned not to ask anyone about anyone else's job. Each of them were very quick to remind me of their particular area of expertise. All were pleasant to work with, though, which frankly surprised me. For some reason, I suspected they might act snooty, working for the President and all, but nothing could have been further from the truth. Advance Team members took the time to explain to me, as they went along, why something had to be a certain way. Of course, I argued on several occasions that this and that made no sense and I even won a few. Knowing our Media Center as I did, I thought getting it ready for a presidential visit was virtually an impossible task. At the time, I guess I was thinking about *me* trying to get that job done, not the President's team trying to get the job done.

For several days to follow, it was the invasion of the black suits. All of them wore dark colored suits. My children wanted to know who the men in black were, but I couldn't say a thing at that point.

I was told to say nothing, and I can truly say, for the first time in my life, I was quiet. It was like getting a five carat engagement ring from a married man and not being able to show it to anyone. Yeah, you can take it out of the box when no one is around, even slip it on your finger. Sharing it with people you know and love, however, is out of the question.

I realize a host of things now that I did not thoroughly understand as I was first going into the whole security thing. Talk about attention to detail—again I now know of its relevant importance. At that point, we were still two days into the Advance Team's visit, and they were still combing and sweeping the campus. No decision had yet been made whether the president would even visit our school, but I was loving the journey. Still, nothing had been changed, nothing moved. Let me remind you again our Media Center is filled with used display cases, tables, chairs, computers, televisions, books, and plenty of bookshelves. On Friday, August 31, the decision was made. It was official. He was coming! I actually heard it on the five o'clock news. I called to confirm its authenticity. Yes, the President was officially slated to come to The Emma!

Up until this time, the Advance Team had reminded me that no selection had been made. Now that our school had been selected, I was told it was not a sure thing the President would show up. It depended on how busy he was or something to that effect.

Once the word got out about our selection, I was contacted by two principals, one from Sarasota and one from out of state. Both of them shared their experiences. They had been told the President was coming to their schools, but something happened and he never made it. They told me not get too caught up in the moment or I may be disappointed later. I didn't want to hear it or hear of it. If the POTUS says he was coming, he'd better be making his way to The Emma. Every time I had a discussion with any of the President's security people, I told them he would never be the same after he experienced Emma E. Booker Elementary.

It was Friday, August 31. None of the President's people around the school looked familiar to me. Each day, it seemed like I was seeing more and more new faces. Still, nothing had been moved.

Suddenly, one familiar face appeared, and a series of questions were asked regarding moving things around and the movement of the President during his visit. In the next 48 hours I saw my Media Center transformed. I became quite busy—there's a lot to do in getting ready for a visit from the President once your school's been selected.

Everybody was working behind the scenes to lend me support. Sheila stayed with me the entire time and was working her area. I was working with her on the infamous list, which turned out not to be much of a list at all. People were invited who I had never seen before. The space we had to work with was limited, the number of people wanting to be invited was large, so in order not to offend anyone, it was a closed ceremony. It was opened only to the staff, a few parents, a group of students, and my pastor, Neville Gritt.

I had to invite Neville because he loved the President. Of my entire circle of friends, he was the person I knew who I thought would enjoy meeting the President the most.

It's amazing how many people you know when something really big is happening. I had to ask myself, Wouldn't I be doing the same thing trying to get into such an historic event? It's the American way.

It was made easy for me. No invitations could be sent out. My pastor and the principal's shared decision making/planning and management team were my only invitations. Frankly, I was glad. It was going to be ugly otherwise. I could feel the tension mounting with those who thought they should be in attendance, but it was fair and equitable. No one received invitations.

The Advance Team must have known my mother. Mothers are probably the one reason they said *tell no one*. A dad would be proud and probably quite cool about the whole thing, but a mother... that's a whole other story. As soon as I was able to tell my mother what was happening, she told the state of Indiana and probably did a fair job of calling most of the people in the state of Virginia as well.

Let's go back to the Media Center—today is Friday—we are filling in the details and I see the impossible getting done: phone lines, cables, a communication center is being constructed before my very eyes.

I call my staff together for the second time to tell them that it's official. The Emma has been selected. They are all being invited but there are some specific things they would have to do if they were interested in being considered as audience members or backdrops.

On Tuesday, letters went home with a select group of fourth and fifth grade leadership students informing their parents of a meeting Sunday at 2 p.m. in the cafeteria. The purpose of the meeting would be to explain all the details, step by step, of what would occur during the President's visit. The letter encouraged parents to arrive early for the meeting with their students, then expect to wait, and park and shuttle. No cars would be allowed to park in our parking lot. Parents and students needed to prepare to be searched and know that they would be going through a metal detector.

Even though I had written the letter to the parents on official Emma E. Booker stationery with my official Rigell signature, it was still unbelievable to most of them. After filtering many, and I do mean *many*, calls people began to believe. Hadn't they seen the news? Some said that they had. Others, well, you know the story. Just like in every school, I have some very informed and involved parents, and I have some who think they are part of the first group. Some rely on the children to keep them informed, and some haven't been on campus since the first day of school. It's okay, though, because it's still our job to educate both students and parents, if they're willing to be taught.

Sunday, September 9, arrived and my prayers had been more than answered. Not only had everyone shown up, but we were able to start on time. There was discussion, more discussion, questions, more questions, and finally answers. I could feel tension, excitement, even some fear. Then the meeting was over.

At this point, I needed some time to find the perfect outfit, get my hair and nails done, match my makeup. I was allotted the same 24 hours that everyone else got, which at the time seemed so unfair.

On Monday, September 10, the school was turned upside down and spun around. The transformation was beginning. Remember, I told you our Media Center was packed. Well, it wasn't on Monday. Pack elves had come over the weekend, packed and stacked, then crated all our stuff off to the sides.

You had to be there to see the magnitude of what had just taken place. The Advanced Team had stepped back, and now there were new men and a woman or two at work. The old team hadn't gone away; they'd just faded into the background.

Everybody, and I do mean *everybody*, had kicked into high gear and was jamming right along. Hammers and nails were making their combined noises, pavement was being pounded, and people were moving out. The campus was being raked and scraped. It was exciting just to watch everyone work. Flower beds were being mulched, sod was being laid, trees were getting trimmed, carpets shampooed. A dab of paint was applied here and there. The elves were in overdrive and working overtime with no intention of stopping until the job was done. It went nonstop all day.

I met with the people from the White House Staff over and over that day. They were putting the finishing touches on the order in which things would happen during the President's visit, who would be responsible for doing what, where I should stand.

Let's walk through it again, Ms. Rigell. The car pulls up, you meet him there, make no sudden moves or gestures; introduce him to the person to your right. I went through it over and over. I had my role down.

The White House Staff set up shop in my front office, just across the way from my office. I was informed that if one particular phone rang, I was not to answer it. That phone had become the official White House phone. I jokingly told them, "If the phone rings and no one's around and I'm here, I'll be answering it."

Late that Monday afternoon, I watched the motorcycle escort patrol practice their entry to the school grounds. They looked important as they rounded the end of the parking lot and headed towards the President's stopping point in front of the school.

I went back into my office to work on the few words I would say when welcoming the President. I sat and sat and sat some more. Nothing came. I couldn't think of even two words to put together. Several people stopped by my office and offered to help me. I kept telling them, "Not yet." Later, the words still would not come.

Through the slats in the blinds in my office, I watched people moving, blueprints in hand, scurrying about. Meanwhile, our art teacher worked endlessly, cranking out banners. The children worked on pictures for the backdrop. The guy in charge of tying it all together was busy doing just that. Each piece worked independently but yet was so much a part of a larger body.

The buses I had requested arrived. They formed a line, bumper to bumper, along the sidewalk in front of the school. Afterwards, people papered the buses' windows. Several times I asked if that was really necessary. I pointed out, "If the buses are here, no one can see through those windows anyway, unless they're in the trees. Why the need for the unsightly paper, then? You're messing with this wonderful ambiance you've just created."

Many times I asked and argued about The Beast (the President's armored limousine) driving up under the alcove near the entrance to the school by the office. At first it seemed like a swell idea. Then I found out approximately how heavy The Beast was. I could just see the little paver bricks popping up under the excessive weight of The Beast.

I thought it would be good for the President to walk those few steps from the sidewalk to the welcome line. The President's people had to convince me otherwise. They also continued to remind me that anything not taken back to its original state would be brought back up to standard, but I knew my government. *When* is always an issue with me. How timely they might be in putting things back to standard is what concerned me a little.

I tried to ask all of the right questions. I've learned from my 13-year- old son, Stevenson, that if you want the answer that you're looking for and believe to be correct, you must ask the right question.

Finally, I had to leave. The Media Center was practically transformed, but yet to be completed. Completed or not, I had to get to my hair appointment or my stylist needed to get to me. Since this was such a special event, she agreed to meet at my house late—and at this point it was getting late. There would be no time for shopping or nails.

She finally showed up. It was a simple hairstyle, something that even I can manage on my own. She reminded me that she was a beautician and not a magician and she'd do her best to make it hold. She sprayed it down until you could actually bounce things off my hair. I actually wanted to sleep standing up not to interfere with the wonderful job she had done. She literally did surgery on my hair. If you're reading this book and you're a woman, you know the effects of humidity on hair. If it's black hair, humidity really does a number on it.

It was my intention to get to bed early, but I never made it. I spent a little more time trying to think of words, good words to say when welcoming the President and his guests. I said some words over and over again, but I couldn't get anything good enough to put down on paper. Finally, I gave up and went to bed, relying on the fact that my Father God provides for me in any and every situation.

I tried everything, but sleep would not come. Chamomile tea, Sleepy Time tea, the ocean waves, still no sleep. Then I remembered my secret weapon. I'm almost ashamed to admit, but whenever I can't sleep, I lie in bed and pray that that old Devil rushes me to sleep quickly. I gave my secret weapon a try that night. That was the last thing I remember until the 5 a.m. wake–up call.

Emma E. Booker Elementary School
September 11, 2001

PATRIOT DAY, 2002

By the President of the United States of America

A Proclamation

On this first observance of Patriot Day, we remember and honor those who perished in the terrorist attacks of September 11, 2001. We will not forget the events of that terrible morning nor will we forget how Americans responded in New York City, at the Pentagon, and in the skies over Pennsylvania--with heroism and selflessness; with compassion and courage; and with prayer and hope. We will always remember our collective obligation to ensure that justice is done, that freedom prevails, and that the principles upon which our Nation was founded endure.

Inspired by the heroic sacrifices of our firefighters, rescue and law enforcement personnel, military service members, and other citizens, our Nation found unity, focus, and strength. We found healing in the national outpouring of compassion for those lost, as tens of millions of Americans participated in moments of silence, candlelight vigils, and religious services. From the tragedy of September 11 emerged a stronger Nation, renewed by a spirit of national pride and a true love of country.

We are a people dedicated to the triumph of freedom and democracy over evil and tyranny. The heroic stories of the first responders who gave their all to save others strengthened our resolve. And our Armed Forces have pursued the war against terrorism in Afghanistan and elsewhere with valor and skill. Together with our coalition partners, they have achieved success.

Americans also have fought back against terror by choosing to overcome evil with good. By loving their neighbors as they would like to be loved, countless citizens have answered the call to help others. They have contributed to relief efforts, improved homeland security in their communities, and volunteered their time to aid those in need. This spirit of service continues to grow as thousands have joined the newly established USA Freedom Corps, committing themselves to changing America one heart at a time through the momentum of millions of acts of decency and kindness.

Those whom we lost last September 11 will forever hold a cherished place in our hearts and in the history of our Nation. As we mark the first anniversary of that tragic day, we remember their sacrifice; and we commit ourselves to honoring their memory by pursuing peace and justice in the world and security at home. By a joint resolution approved December 18, 2001 (Public Law 107-89), the Congress has authorized and requested the President to designate September 11 of each year as "Patriot Day."

NOW, THEREFORE, I, GEORGE W. BUSH, President of the United States of America, do hereby proclaim September 11, 2002, as Patriot Day. I call upon the people of the United States to observe this day with appropriate ceremonies and activities, including remembrance services and candlelight vigils. I also call upon the Governors of the United States and the Commonwealth of Puerto Rico, as well as appropriate officials of all units of government, to direct that the flag be flown at half-staff on Patriot Day. Further, I encourage all Americans to display the flag at half-staff from their homes on that day and to observe a moment of silence beginning at 8:46 a.m. eastern daylight time, or another appropriate commemorative time, to honor the innocent victims who lost their lives as a result of the terrorist attacks of September 11, 2001.

IN WITNESS WHEREOF, I have hereunto set my hand this fourth day of September, in the year of our Lord two thousand two, and of the Independence of the United States of America the two hundred and twenty-seventh.

George Bush

As our nation copes with the horrible tragedies of the terrorist attacks on September 11th, please continue to pray for the families and loved ones of the victims.

May God bless them all, and may God bless America.

THE WHITE HOUSE

WASHINGTON

September 17, 2001

Emma E. Booker Elementary School
2350 Dr. Martin Luther King, Jr. Way
Sarasota, Florida 34234

To My Friends at Emma Booker Elementary School:

Thank you for inviting me to come to your school last week. I enjoyed my visit and really appreciate your understanding why it was important for me to leave early.

Mrs. Bush and I hope you have a great school year and that you always remember to study hard and read a lot!

Sincerely,

George W. Bush

THE WHITE HOUSE

WASHINGTON

September 17, 2001

Ms. Gwen Rigell
Principal
Emma E. Booker Elementary School
2350 Dr. Martin Luther King, Jr. Way
Sarasota, Florida 34234

Dear Gwen:

Please accept my sincere apologies that my visit to your school was cut short by the horrible tragedies of last week's terrorist attacks. I hope that I will have a chance to visit again someday.

In the meantime, thank you for all that you and your team are doing to help make sure that every child receives a good education. You are making a real difference!

I appreciate as well everything you are doing to help children understand the horrible tragedies of last week's terrorist attacks. I know you join Laura and me in praying for the victims and their families. May God bless them, and may God bless America.

Sincerely,

George W. Bush

Part 2

September 11, 2001

Tuesday morning, September 11, one minute after five. I wanted to lie in bed a little longer, but I remembered all that I had to do, why and where I needed to be, and I knew I needed to be there early.

I dragged my son out of bed. Stevenson wasn't thrilled about getting up early and riding into work with me, but I was a single parent and the options were few. He had no choice, grumpy and all, but to roll out of bed and start his day much earlier than he was accustomed to.

As I was getting dressed, I prayed that things would go smoothly. I prayed for the President's protection and that nothing would happen to him while he was entrusted to my care.

Stevenson had been allowed to sleep until the very last minute, but it still wasn't good enough. Remember it wasn't Santa or Jackie Chan. I said all the words like this is a once in a lifetime event, and how many children, let alone adults, could ever say they were in the same small room with the President? Trust me, my pep talk didn't help him get dressed any faster.

My hair survived the night but there wasn't enough hair spray to provide the fortress it would need for the takeover siege of humidity. It was now just after 6 a.m., and I swear I was tired already. I still had no words written, and this was the one event I didn't want to ad-lib. Again I prayed that all would go well with the President's visit.

Of all the clothes in my closet, nothing seemed to work. Last night the suit seemed perfect. This morning it wasn't working for me. It would just have to do. I could already feel my make-up melting down.

Finally, Stevenson and I were in the car where the air conditioner was up close and personal. Of course, Stevenson complained that it was too cold (nobody could be that hot), but I drove on in silence. He really didn't want to hear what I was thinking at that moment. I was still trying hard to formulate a welcome of some kind... still nothing came to me.

My car was the one vehicle that could park in its regular space at the school that morning. Being an administrator, at least for that day, did have its privileges.

I arrived with an agenda in my head. The morning quickly became, however, like every other morning. I walk in and people need stuff. My plan had been to sit at my desk in the silent atmosphere until I was able to come up with my welcoming remarks.

So much for my plan. It didn't last too long at all. People started to gather at the back of the campus without picture identification and no one had any idea who was to be admitted. I left the solitude of my office to be an identifier and pass out badges to those who were to be admitted. The badges later became collectables. Not knowing what incredible events would transpire that particular day, some nice people, me included, gave badges to staff members who didn't get a memento. Finally, the ins were in and the outs were out. The staff, students, media, local Republicans, school board members, parents, and a few honored guests were admitted into the staging area.

What many people don't realize is that there were a lot of people in the Media Center and very little space. It was standing-room only, with the limited seating room reserved for dignitaries. There wasn't much room to move around, and there was only one restroom and one water fountain for more than 200 people.

Everyone was amazed at the students' behaviors inside the staging area. They waited patiently for an audience with the President. My son waited for two hours as well, nowhere near my supervision. Like the rest of his classmates, his behavior rose above the bar.

I stood just inside the main office door, waiting for my signal to come forward, staying there far past the time they wanted me to come out. They didn't know it at the time, but I had no intention of coming out and standing on the sidewalk waiting for the President's arrival.

I understand restricted movement and all of that, but they didn't understand that my hair had no conscience. President or not, it wasn't standing for the heat. All the hairspray in the world wouldn't have helped. It was hot and muggy even though it was considered the cool part of this September day in Florida. Running around the campus at warp speed hadn't made my hair any better either.

I finally said point blank, "You don't understand black hair. If anybody's going to see me with the President, it's going to be with my hair in flip, not flop."

I got the last minute call to come and stand on my little spot. The President was coming! I was on my way out, and still no words had come. For some reason, I had a peace about it. I knew that God had carried me through many difficult situations and brought me through in grand fashion. This would be no different. I had to trust Him.

I asked the Lord if this great experience could possibly be my treat for my bout with cancer. He is a God of the impossible, and all this seemed impossible. All of it. Just think, I told myself, the President would be arriving at The Emma in a few minutes, and I would be the only one from the school district who would get to spend a few moments alone with him. I thought for sure they would want the superintendent of schools. No, they wanted me. I would get the chance to be in the holding room alone with him, where I would give him a quick rundown of my moment of pride. I could highlight whatever I wanted during that time. I thought I'd have his ear for a few minutes.

I was out in the lineup on the sidewalk with the handful of people who were invited to be part of the official greeting committee. I waited. They assured me it wouldn't be more than a few minutes because the President is always quite punctual. I had no idea who many of the people waiting with me were. I stood next to Edwina Oliver who stood next to Sarasota Superintendent Wilma Hamilton. I would have to look at a photo to be able to tell you who stood down the line.

Before President Bush arrived, Lieutenant Governor Brogan was wandering around creating mischief, being his usual gregarious self. He worked the crowd, darting about, even entertaining the teachers and students in the second-grade classroom the President was scheduled to visit. Finally, the long black heavy limousine approached. I watched it turn its way up on my paver bricks, listening to hear if there was a *pop*. I watched as The Beast came to a halt. The door opened and someone ushered the President out. He stepped forward, larger than life, but not much shorter than I expected him to be.

He walked up to me, called me by name, and told me he had to go in and call Condoleezza Rice. I could have sworn I heard him say *Candy.* I was hungry and candy sounded good to me.

Within minutes he returned and picked up right where he'd left off. Hunger or nervousness must have overtaken me for a moment. I forgot my own name and introduced myself as the person I was to introduce to him. I rapidly made the correction and moved on.

Following our cue, the group departed to the Media Center, and President Bush and I walked into the holding room. There were quite a number of people in the room, each looking more important than the next. Soon after entering the room, President Bush turned to me and told me that a commercial plane had hit the World Trade Center. I got the impression from him that it was an accident. He told me, *We will go on.*

Yes, there was a television in the holding room. No, it was not on while I was in there with the President. We chatted very briefly, a few photos were snapped, and we were off to the classroom.

We walked into Mrs. Kay Daniel's second-grade classroom as it has been shown on the TV screen and the movie screen in *Fahrenheit 9-11.* I introduced the President and had all the students stand up to greet the 43rd President of the United States.

Over and over I had been drilled about every detail of the event. The car will pull up. He'll come over and greet the sidewalk guests, go into the holding room, and you alone will accompany him and talk a few minutes about The Emma. You'll walk into the second-grade class and introduce the President. The teachers will have the children stand, lead him to the courtyard to greet more children, shake a few hands and onto the Media Center/staging area to address his reading initiative. Nowhere did it say that Andrew Card would interrupt the children's reading, Rod Paige would address the school, and Frank Brogan would be in charge. Things changed quickly.

Part 3

Final Thoughts

Seven minutes are still in question. It's what all the debates and discussions have been about, so here is my take on that. As I have stated previously, I'm not a politician. I have nothing to promote nor any political ax to grind.

It's my account of the events that took place on that day and a person's behavior. I am as qualified as anyone to make an assessment of the behavior, it just so happened that this person was the President and happens to be a Republican. No, for the thousandth time, I am not a Republican but from where I stood, his behavior was commendable. With my own eyes, I witnessed something, what I wasn't quite sure of, but it didn't follow any briefing I had received. No place in the script said that Andrew Card would walk in front of me in the second-grade classroom and whisper something to the President.

At the moment, I didn't know the content of the conversation, but I did see the change in the President's countenance. He heard something and responded rather than reacted. I know he went somewhere for a brief moment and returned. He returned stronger and confident. I watched President Bush as he emerged as a leader.

For just a moment he bit the ends of his lip, just where the mouth curls up on the ends. He leaned over, picked up the book, *The Pet Goat*, and followed the children as they read the story. No, it is not a single story in a book you buy at a bookstore; it's a story in a basal reader, part of a reading series. He appeared to listen, but you could tell his mind was somewhere else.

When the last child read the words, "to be continued," the President's response was, "What does it mean *to be continued*?" A child answered, "It means there is more to come." "That's right," both the teacher and the President responded. At that point, the President said his brief goodbyes. Just as I was about to escort him to the next station, he informed me that there had been a change in plans. America was under attack, and it was believed to be terrorist in nature. He apologized for having to leave so abruptly. I heard what he was telling me, but nothing really registered. For a moment I stood there, feet planted in time, mind racing, trying to make some sense of what it all meant. My brain was engaged, going nowhere and everywhere all at the same time. What did he mean by *terrorist in nature*? Yes, I know what terrorism means, but not in America. This is a free country, and we are free to move around as we like, free from fear. I knew enough to know that a war of some kind would follow.

Let me not again get ahead of what happened. Many times since that day I have been asked why he stayed. Why didn't I feel he should have left immediately? Wasn't the President endangering the children by not leaving immediately?

What impressed me most was that the President sat, listened, addressed the children, and moved on to address the nation. He didn't listen to Andrew Card's words, then jump up and knock a chair over trying to get out of the room.

Yes, he stayed. He gathered himself and his thoughts as the people who worked behind the scenes gathered information. It would have served little or no purpose for him to have heard the word and dismissed himself from the room. Nothing could have or would have happened any more expeditiously.

Yes, a horrific thing had occurred, but let's look at what the terrorists wanted to have happen. They wanted America to be stunned. They wanted to cripple America, and they wanted to see fear on the face of the President. It didn't happen. I've said repeatedly that I didn't vote for him, but I could have on that day. I could not have been prouder of the man. He emerged looking quite presidential.

There was little opportunity for anyone to feed him a response, he was up there in front of the nation, and then he was gone. He was a different man by the time he left.

How can we argue that America was not better for the moment? We were strong for the moment, scared, but brave. Seven minutes––that's what it comes down to. The seven minutes from the time Andrew Card whispered in the President's ear until the time the President left the school. We're hanging the future of what America is and what America represents on seven minutes. Don't be distracted. The President is the final word, but he is not the beginning. Every agency that could have been at work was at work during those seven minutes; don't discount the power of America.

While he sat thinking of the steps to take, nothing was lost. Common sense is neither Democratic nor Republican. It's available to all who choose to pursue it. I, too, am a great Monday morning quarterback. It's easy for me to see clearly what plays should have been called after the game is over. When the pressure is on, the time allowed to make a decision is quite different.

We are known for reacting; this time there was a response to the actions taken against America. The words were simple yet profound:

"Ladies and Gentlemen, this is a difficult moment for America. I unfortunately will be going back to Washington after my remarks. Secretary Rod Paige and the Lieutenant Governor will take the podium and discuss education. I do want to thank the folks here at Booker Elementary School for their hospitality."

The end was really the beginning. All the phone calls started. First, parents wanting to know if school was dismissed and if the school was safe. All the phone lines were tied up. There was a media frenzy. Everyone was trying to get their story out. Every reporter was determined to go live from The Emma.

The President left, but no one else was going anywhere. Grounded reporters can be a scary thing. Their frenzy, however, was short-lived. A local reporter appealed to her colleagues, requesting they have respect for the students, staff, and parents at our school. A lot had gone on that day and the less said with regards to the children the better.

Many interviews were granted. People from around the country called—from magazines, newspapers, television stations, television shows, and radio stations. Then, other countries began calling.

Jeffrey Rosenberg has been, by far, the most accurate in his account of what happened at The Emma that day. Only a few others have come close. Most reported what they wanted to say, it certainly isn't what I said. I received many hate e-mails and vicious letters. I also got many wonderful letters and calls.

Words are so powerful, they are so important in the creation of views that support a detailed picture. My picture for hours lacked much of the supporting details. It wasn't until long after the planes had struck the towers, the Pennsylvania field, and the Pentagon, that I actually viewed the footage. No string of words could have prepared me for what I was about to view.

People kept telling me that a plane hit or struck the towers. I had been to those towers many, many times. I stood out on the top, viewed the city, and felt their strength. These words conjured a piece of the building missing, a corner knocked off or maybe some concrete missing—nothing close to the magnitude of what I was to see when I walked into my office. My eyes were not able to prepare my brain for the scrambled message; sure I saw the pictures yet my experiences overrode what my brain configured. For a moment, I had to shut down and repair my head. Every target was a familiar picture. How can you separate a vision that is so unreal?

Our school will never be the same, as a country our lives will never be the same, and, as a people, I hope to God we will change. This is our chance. Let us seize this opportunity. Let us return to the foundation, the very roots and principles this country was established under.

Printed by Libri Plureos GmbH in Hamburg,
Germany